NEW STUDIES IN

ETHICAL NATURALISM

Ethical Naturalism: Hobbes and Hume

J. KEMP, M.A.
Professor of Philosophy
University of Leicester

MACMILLAN
ST MARTIN'S PRESS

© J. Kemp 1970

First published 1970 *by*
MACMILLAN AND CO LTD
Little Essex Street London W C 2
and also at Bombay Calcutta and Madras
Macmillan South Africa (Publishers) Pty Ltd Johannesburg
The Macmillan Company of Australia Pty Ltd Melbourne
The Macmillan Company of Canada Ltd Toronto
St Martin's Press Inc New York
Gill and Macmillan Ltd Dublin

Library of Congress catalog card no. 78–108404

Printed in Great Britain by
RICHARD CLAY (THE CHAUCER PRESS) LTD
Bungay, Suffolk

FOR MY WIFE

CONTENTS

EDITOR'S PREFACE

New Studies in Ethics is a series of monographs, written by philosophers drawn from universities in Great Britain, the United States and Australia. The aim of the series is to provide a comprehensive survey of the main types of ethical theory from the point of view of contemporary analytical philosophy.

In the present volume, Professor Kemp introduces ethical naturalism through the work of two of the most influential of British philosophers. He places the philosophy of Hobbes and Hume in its contemporary setting and seeks to understand it sympathetically. His aim is to show precisely what views Hobbes and Hume held respectively, and to bring out what is of continuing interest and significance in their work. The is–ought question, which arises in connection with the moral philosophy of both Hobbes and Hume, is still one of the central problems, if not the central problem, in that subject.

Professor Kemp's expositions are clear and his criticisms incisive. His *Study* will provide a useful introduction to an important part of Ethics for undergraduates studying that subject; but it will be of interest also to those more widely read in moral philosophy.

University of Exeter   W. D. HUDSON

REFERENCES

HOBBES

Leviathan *Leviathan or the Matter, Forme and Power of a Commonwealth Ecclesiasticall and Civil* by Thomas Hobbes. Edited with an Introduction by Michael Oakeshott (Oxford, n.d.).

EW *The English Works of Thomas Hobbes* collected and edited by Sir William Molesworth, 11 vols (London, 1839–45).

LW *Thomae Hobbes – Opera Philosophica quae Latine scripsit* collecta studio et labore Gulielmi Molesworth, 5 vols (London, 1839–45).

HUME

T *A Treatise of Human Nature.* References are to book, chapter and section, followed by the page in the edition by L. A. Selby-Bigge (Oxford, 1888).

EM *An Inquiry concerning the Principals of Morals.* References are to section and part, followed by (i) the page in the edition by C. W. Hendel (Library of Liberal Arts, Indianapolis, 1957) and (ii) the page in the edition of *Hume's Enquiries* by L. A. Selby-Bigge (Oxford, 1902).

I. INTRODUCTION

The use of such general descriptive words or labels as 'Naturalism', 'Realism' and 'Idealism' can hardly be avoided in writing the history of philosophy, but it can sometimes be misleading. Philosophy is written by individuals, not by schools or groups. Labels, where they are correctly and sensibly applied, are signs of resemblances and affinities between the various things to which any one label is affixed; but those resemblances and affinities are not the whole story, and not all naturalists or realists or idealists give identical answers to identical questions. It is especially important to guard against the danger of wrongly reading back into history the disputes and arguments of one's own day; however understandable may be the desire to strengthen one's own case by finding it anticipated in the work of one's most distinguished predecessors, the history of philosophy repeats itself no more exactly than the history of any other human activity. The philosophical views and arguments discussed in this essay were not designed, and should not on the whole be interpreted, as contributions to the twentieth-century debate on ethical naturalism which was initiated by G. E. Moore's supposed discovery of the Naturalistic Fallacy (in *Principia Ethica*, first published in 1903). I have therefore tried for the most part to expound them in relation to the questions which their authors were trying to answer, rather than distort them by picturing them as answers to questions which concern us in our own present debates.

In treating of the ethical naturalism of the seventeenth and eighteenth centuries, I have thought it best to concentrate, in the small space at my disposal, on the two major figures of Hobbes (1588–1679) and Hume (1711–76) rather than try to deal, in a necessarily cursory way, with lesser writers as well; and in discussing Hobbes I have, for a similar reason, concentrated on the theory of *Leviathan* (published in 1651) and said little about the views, in some respects very different, of the *Elements of Law* (published in manuscript form in 1640) or the *De Cive* (published in 1642). The *Leviathan* is not merely Hobbes's masterpiece but is also, more specifically, the work in which he produces the most thoroughly painstaking and systematic arguments. If the attempt in *Leviathan* to draw practical conclusions from premisses about the nature of the universe and of man does not succeed, we shall certainly not find a more successful attempt elsewhere in his writings. As far as Hume is concerned, I have tried to take adequate account of both the *Treatise of Human Nature* (books I and II published in 1739, book III in 1740) and of the *Enquiry concerning the Principles of Morals* (1751).

II. HOBBES

(i) THE MATHEMATICAL AND SCIENTIFIC BACKGROUND

In the Epistle Dedicatory to the *De Corpore*, dated 23 April
1655, Hobbes makes some remarks which give us an interesting
indication of the way in which he regarded the development of
science, or Philosophy, and his own contributions to it. The
ancients, he concedes, achieved important results in geometry and
logic, put forward the hypothesis of the earth's diurnal motion,
and made some discoveries in astronomy. But while the geometrical and logical achievements remained accessible, the physical
and astronomical discoveries did not, being, as Hobbes puts it,
'by succeeding philosophers strangled with the snares of words'
(*EW* i viii). 'And therefore the beginning of astronomy, except
observations, I think is not to be derived from farther time than
from Nicolaus Copernicus; who in the age next preceding the present revived the opinion of Pythagoras, Aristarchus, and Philolaus.'
Galileo is then mentioned as the real founder of natural philosophy:
'After him [Copernicus], the doctrine of the motion of the earth
being now received, and a difficult question thereupon arising
concerning the descent of heavy bodies, Galileus in our time,
striving with that difficulty, was the first that opened to us the
gate of natural philosophy universal, which is the knowledge of
the nature of *motion*. So that neither can the age of natural philosophy be reckoned higher than to him.' Finally, the science of
human physiology ('the science of *man's body*, the most profitable
part of natural science') has been established by Harvey. Great
progress has since been made in a short time; in astronomy and
natural science by Kepler, Gassendi and Mersenne, in physiology
'by the wit and industry of physicians, the only true natural
philosophers, especially of our most learned men of the College
of Physicians in London' (*EW* i ix). But what of civil, or political,
philosophy? This, Hobbes claims, is a still younger science, 'as

being no older (I say it provoked, and that my detractors may know how little they have wrought upon me) than my own book *De Cive*' (ibid.). Of course, there were many before Hobbes who were called political philosophers, but they did not deserve the name. Hobbes's contempt for the 'philosophy' of the Greeks and the medieval scholastics has many grounds; most important for our purpose is his belief that it had no sure foundation and no methodical procedure which would allow for the checking and proving or disproving of conclusions – the result was barren dispute or nonsense, words being used to obscure the truth rather than reveal it.

Now Hobbes's mention of such names as Copernicus, Galileo and Harvey is not an irrelevant catalogue of achievements in a totally different field from his own. Hobbes, like them, is practising philosophy, in the contemporary wide sense of the word, and claims to be achieving a comparable success; there must therefore be some affinities or analogies between his method and theirs. Some of these affinities are procedural, others concern questions of content: to the former group belong the insistence on beginning with precise definitions in order to avoid the twin dangers of confusion and nonsense, and the demand for strict logical argument at every stage; to the latter belong Hobbes's central use of the concepts of body and motion. Aubrey's famous account of Hobbes's discovery of geometry is relevant here:

> Being in a gentleman's library in ——, Euclid's Elements lay open, and 'twas the 47 El. libri 1. 'By G——' sayd he, 'this is impossible!' [He would now and then sweare, by way of emphasis.] So he reads the demonstration of it, which referred him back to such a proposition; which proposition he read. That referred him back to another, which also he read. Et sic deinceps, that at last he was demonstratively convinced of that trueth. This made him in love with geometry. (*Aubrey's Brief Lives 1669–1696*, ed. A. Clark (Oxford, 1898) I 332)

The Latin prose life of Hobbes, written by himself, makes it clear that it was the structure of Euclid's proofs that fascinated him more than their actual geometrical content: 'et delectatus methodo illius [sc. Euclidis], non tam ob theoremata illius, quam ob artem ratiocinandi, diligentissime perlegit' (*LW* I xiv). Geometry is

4

admittedly, for Hobbes, a kind of abstract science of motion, in the sense that all geometrical figures are constructed by the motion of points, lines, etc.; and the concept of motion plays a part in his account of human psychology as well as in that of physics and physiology – appetites and aversions are, quite literally, motions (though of a rather special kind). Nevertheless, the main importance of geometry, and of mathematics in general, to Hobbes's moral and political philosophy is its impact on his method of argument. Large parts of his work purport to consist of conclusions drawn by strict ratiocination from properly established premisses (these premisses consisting of propositions whose terms are clearly defined).

> Seeing then that truth consisteth in the right ordering of names in our affirmations, a man that seeketh precise truth had need to remember what every name he uses stands for, and to place it accordingly, or else he will find himself entangled in words, as a bird in lime twigs, the more he struggles the more belimed. And therefore in geometry, which is the only science that it hath pleased God hitherto to bestow on mankind, men begin at settling the significations of their words; which settling of significations they call *definitions*, and place them in the beginning of their reckoning. (*Leviathan* 21)

Hobbes believes that the failure to begin with definitions is responsible for most of the absurdities of what passes for political philosophy. Writers use and combine words and phrases into sentences that are quite literally meaningless, although their meaninglessness escapes the notice of those who fail to ask for definitions. If a man began to talk about circular quadrilaterals (to adapt one of Hobbes's own examples) he could easily be shown to be talking nonsense; reference to the Euclidean definitions of 'circle' and 'quadrilateral' would clearly show the mutual incompatibility of the two concepts. Yet scholastic philosophers (and their later followers) talk quite happily about something called 'inpoured virtue' or 'incorporeal substance', although if we insist on the relevant terms being defined we shall discover an equally decisive incompatibility. Another important cause of misunderstanding and confusion, which the practice of definition can remove, is the use of words which mean different things in different contexts; a confusion which,

Hobbes thinks, is especially likely to arise in those matters in which men's judgments are most affected by their passions.

And therefore in reasoning a man must take heed of words; which besides the signification of what we imagine of their nature, have a signification also of the nature, disposition, and interest of the speaker; such as are the names of virtues and vices; for one man calleth *wisdom*, what another calleth *fear*; and one *cruelty*, what another *justice*; one *prodigality*, what another *magnanimity*; and one *gravity*, what another *stupidity*, &c. And therefore such names can never be true grounds of any ratiocination. (*Leviathan* 24–5)

This last point is especially important for moral, or civil, philosophy. It is no use thinking that we can establish stable and objective criteria of conduct by drawing up lists of virtues and vices in accordance with the common usage of the relevant terms; for this common usage has itself no stability or objectivity – a point which Hobbes develops further in connection with his account of the nature of appetite and aversion, the basic causes of human action. There are, he says, two kinds of motion peculiar to animals: vital motion and animal, or voluntary, motion. Vital motions are those which take place without the need of any thought or imagination: the circulation of the blood, breathing, nutritional processes, and so on. Voluntary motion, on the other hand (for example, speaking and moving our limbs), requires preceding thought: before speaking we think in imagination of what we are going to say, before walking anywhere we think in imagination of our destination. It is an important feature of Hobbes's account of voluntary motion (and so of voluntary action in general) that the initial setting oneself to act is itself, or involves, motion, even though at this stage the motion is too small to be perceptible to observation: 'these small beginnings of motion, within the body of man, before they appear in walking, speaking, striking, and other visible actions, are commonly called ENDEAVOUR' (*Leviathan* 31). There are two primary kinds of endeavour, appetite or desire, and aversion, the former being endeavour (i.e. imperceptible motion) towards the object that causes it, the latter endeavour away from its cause. All appetite and love are accompanied by some delight, or pleasure: all aversion and hate by some displeasure. (Note that Hobbes's view, in *Leviathan* at least, is not a kind of hedonism. A man feels pleasure at the thought of his appetite for, or 'motion towards', the desired object and displeasure at that of his aversion for the repellent one; i.e. pleasure and displeasure are secondary phenomena, not the primary causes of voluntary action.) Human nature is such that of itself it provides no stability or structure to a man's appetites and aversions, still less any mutual coherence between the desires of one man and those of another. 'And because the constitution of a man's body is in continual mutation, it is impossible that all the same things should always cause in him the same appetites, and aversions: much less can all men consent, in the desire of almost any one and the same object.

(ii) GOOD AND EVIL AND THE ORIGINS OF POLITICAL SOCIETY

But whatsoever is the object of any man's appetite or desire, that is it which he for his part calleth *good*: and the object of his hate and aversion, *evil*; and of his contempt, *vile* and *inconsiderable*. For these words of good, evil and contemptible, are ever used with relation to the person that useth them: there being nothing simply and absolutely so; nor any common rule of good and evil, to be taken from the nature of the objects themselves' (*Leviathan* 32). This passage is frequently quoted by writers on Hobbes, and is almost as frequently mistaken for his last, as well as his first, word on the subject of good and evil. If we look at the immediately following phrases, however, we shall see that the situation is not quite as simple as this: 'but from the person of the man, where there is no commonwealth; or, in a commonwealth, from the person that representeth it; or from an arbitrator or judge, whom men disagreeing shall by consent set up, and make his sentence the rule thereof' (*Leviathan* 32–3). And in a passage near the end of *Leviathan* Hobbes explicitly criticises those thinkers whose whole account of good and evil is determined by reference to the desires of the individual man: 'Aristotle, and other heathen philosophers, define good and evil, by the appetite of men; and well enough, as long as we consider them governed every one by his own law; for in the condition of men that have no other law but their own appetites, there can be no general rule of good, and evil actions. But in a commonwealth this measure is false: not the appetite of private men, but the law, which is the will and appetite of the state, is the measure' (*Leviathan* 446). Of course, even in commonwealths many individuals do govern their actions solely by reference to their own private appetites and aversions, and use the words 'good' and 'evil' accordingly. But this is not how men ought to act: 'this private measure of good, is a doctrine, not only vain, but also pernicious to the public state' (ibid.).

But what exactly is the force of this 'ought', and how, given Hobbes's initial assumptions about the nature and causes of voluntary action, is it possible for us to argue from a position in which a man simply satisfies, or attempts to satisfy, each and every appetite and aversion as it occurs, to a conclusion that he ought to respect and obey rules of conduct laid down by authority on behalf of the whole community? In spite of the language which Hobbes sometimes uses, this is not an historical question; it is of no great importance to Hobbes's argument to know whether any men ever did, as a matter of fact, pass from a situation in which each was his own judge of good and evil to one in which each submitted to standards or rules laid down by a central authority. In actual fact indeed, he points out, many commonwealths are formed or enlarged, and many allegiances created, by the adherence to the sovereign of an existing commonwealth of men originally outside it (the extension of sovereignty by conquest or 'acquisition', as opposed to its creation *de novo*). The question which concerns Hobbes is rather: what is the point or justification of men organising themselves into political communities (or of remaining so organised if this is how they find themselves)? Commonwealths are artificial constructions, they do not exist in nature; there must then be factors in human nature which lead to the foundation and continuation of political society. It is not until this point has been elucidated that one can usefully ask for proof that men have an obligation to obey the laws of their country.

An important step on the way to understanding Hobbes's view

of the nature and operation of these factors is the realisation that man (perhaps in this differing from all other animals, and certainly from most) is not simply a vehicle for the occurrence of a succession of mutually unrelated and unrelatable desires and aversions. In general terms, men, unlike animals, possess the faculty of speech: specifically and consequently they can reflect on their own desires and assess both the relative importance of these desires and the relative likelihood or unlikelihood of their being able to satisfy them. The concept of felicity, or happiness, is simply that of 'continual success in obtaining those things which a man from time to time desireth, that is to say, continual prospering' (*Leviathan* 39); and although man, being always in a state of motion, can never be without some unsatisfied desire, nevertheless he can plan his life with a view to the attainment of felicity, i.e. to the satisfaction of the most important, at least, of his wants and desires.

The felicity of this life, consisteth not in the repose of a mind satisfied. For there is no such *finus ultimus*, utmost aim, nor *summum bonum*, greatest good, as is spoken of in the books of the old moral philosophers. Nor can a man any more live, whose desires are at an end, than he, whose senses and imaginations are at a stand. Felicity is a continual progress of the desire, from one object to another; the attaining of the former, being still but the way to the latter. The cause whereof is, that the object of man's desire, is not to enjoy once only, and for one instant of time; but to assure for ever, the way of his future desire. And therefore the voluntary actions, and inclinations of all men, tend, not only to the procuring, but also to the assuring of a contented life. (*Leviathan* 63)

The diversity of human behaviour is partly the result of variations in desires and appetites, partly the result of men's different calculations as to the way in which their desires may best be gratified.

Now if men could achieve both their first-order objectives and the second-order objective of ensuring the conditions necessary for the achievement of the first-order ones, there would be no need for political society; men would live as individuals or in families,[1] each pursuing, and on the whole at least successfully pursuing, the end of obtaining the things he desired and of avoiding the things to which he was averse. In Hobbes's view, however, such a happy state of affairs is impossible. One man's attempt to satisfy his desires and to acquire the power which will enable him to ensure their future satisfaction will inevitably bring him into competition with others; the world is not so constituted that every man can have everything he wants. In particular, a man cannot secure what he has without trying to possess more. 'Competition of riches, honour, command, or other power, inclineth to contention, enmity, and war: because the way of one competitor, to the attaining of his desire, is to kill, subdue, supplant, or repel the other' (*Leviathan* 64). Moreover, men are by nature almost equally endowed with bodily and mental faculties, so that even the apparently weakest and least intelligent will hope on occasion to get the better of the stronger and cleverer; and inferiority on one occasion only may lead to one's death at the hand of an enemy – the stronger cannot rationally console himself with the thought that he will after all win most of his battles if the first lost battle causes him to lose his life. Men are thus naturally enemies to one another because of the need for competition in order to survive, added to the impossibility in these circumstances of trusting anyone else and to the common tendency of men to hate and proceed against those who look down on them. 'So that in the nature of man, we find three principal causes of quarrel. First, competition; secondly, diffidence [sc. distrust]; thirdly, glory. The first maketh men invade for gain; the second, for safety; and the third, for reputation' (*Leviathan* 81).[2]

If, then, we consider men in a condition in which there is no 'common power to keep them all in awe' (*Leviathan* 82), we must conclude that they are in a state of war or enmity with one another (this does not mean, Hobbes is careful to point out, that they are fighting all the time, but that, even when they are not actually fighting, conditions are present that dispose them to fight on the slightest provocation). In this 'state of nature' a man has no security against his enemies beyond that which is provided by his own strength and intelligence; and since every other human being is, at least potentially, his enemy, the degree of security enjoyed by even the strongest and most intelligent man will not be worth much. To quote one of the most famous passages from *Leviathan*:

In such condition, there is no place for industry; because the fruit thereof is uncertain: and consequently no culture of the earth; no navigation, nor use of the commodities that may be imported by sea; no commodious building; no instruments of moving, and removing, such things as require much force; no knowledge of the face of the earth; no account of time; no arts; no letters; no society; and which is worst of all, continual fear, and danger of violent death; and the life of man, solitary, poor, nasty, brutish, and short. (82)

In the state of nature, Hobbes says at one point (though the remark is later given some modification), there is no such thing as right and wrong, or justice and injustice, and no rules of property. Justice and injustice 'are qualities, that relate to men in society, not in solitude' (*Leviathan* 83). But if any men ever were in this sorry condition, how could they improve their situation? Hobbes's answer is partly in terms of men's passions and desires, partly in terms of their rationality or intellectual powers. 'The passions that incline men to peace, are fear of death; desire of such things as are necessary to commodious living; and a hope by their industry to obtain them. And reason suggesteth convenient articles of peace, upon which men may be drawn to agreement. These articles, are they, which otherwise are called the Laws of Nature' (*Leviathan* 84).

If we ignore Hobbes's quasi-historical language, the gist of what he has so far said amounts to this. We find observed or professed in existing human societies rules which prescribe certain kinds of conduct as just or right and forbid other kinds as unjust or wrong. The question arises: what is the status of these rules, and why should men obey them? It is no use saying simply, as far too many so-called philosophers have done, that reason tells us we ought to or that it is natural to men to obey them; the only answer that makes sense is one in terms of human desires – what human desires can be satisfied, and how, by the general observance of a set of rules of conduct that cannot be satisfied in any other way? And when the answer to this question turns out to be that it is only in some kind of artificially constructed society that the peace and security can be achieved which are the necessary conditions for the assured satisfaction of any desires whatsoever, the further question arises: what must the nature of this society be, and what are the principles on which it must be ruled? This last is a question which belongs properly to Hobbes's political philosophy, in the narrow sense of the term, and his detailed answer to it is not our direct concern. It is important, however, to bear in mind that Hobbes's whole argument from the beginning is designed to show, not merely that men cannot lead the kind of lives they want except within the framework of political society, but also, more specifically, that the members of this political society must submit unconditionally to the authority of an absolute sovereign. Moreover, we cannot altogether avoid considering the political element, since for Hobbes moral right and wrong can exist in the fullest sense, at least, only in a political society.

(iii) HOBBES'S ACCOUNT OF NATURAL LAW

A large part of Hobbes's answer to the question how obligation is to be derived from the consideration of human nature is contained in his account of the laws of nature. They have a function in the general structure of his argument very similar to that which they had in earlier, classical, theories of natural law: i.e. that of connecting an account of man's nature with an account of the way in which man, because of this nature, ought to behave. Hobbes's laws are, however, quite unlike the classical laws in a number of ways. He enumerates nineteen such laws in chapters 14 and 15 of *Leviathan*, and adds a twentieth in the 'Review and Conclusion' at the end of the work. The first three, however, are by far the most important and are the only ones that need concern us in any detail.

The first stage in Hobbes's elucidation of the notion of a law of nature consists in his distinguishing it carefully from that of natural right. The right of nature 'is the liberty each man hath, to use his own power, as he will himself, for the preservation of his own nature; that is to say, of his own life; and consequently, of doing any thing, which in his own judgment, and reason, he shall conceive to be the aptest means thereunto' (*Leviathan* 84).

It is important to notice that the word 'right' is being used here in a very different way from that exemplified in such statements as 'Every citizen has a right to a living wage'. In the latter case there is an implication that someone (or perhaps the state) ought to ensure that the citizen gets his rights and that he may legitimately feel aggrieved if he does not; but Hobbes's right of nature carries no comparable implication with it. It means no more than that a man may legitimately (i.e. without incurring any complaint that his action is morally or otherwise wrong) take the steps which he thinks necessary to the preservation of his own life;[3] it does not mean that one man in a state of nature has any sort of duty or obligation to protect the natural right of another. A law of nature, however, requires a certain kind of conduct – it does not merely permit it: 'A Law of Nature is a precept or general rule, found out by reason, by which a man is forbidden to do that, which is destructive of his life, or taketh away the means of preserving the same; and to omit that, by which he thinketh it may be best preserved' (*Leviathan* 84). Now we have seen that in a state of nature it may be a necessary condition of a man's survival and of the satisfaction of any of his desires that he should use force or violence against each other men who stand between him and the achievement of his purpose; and this may be summed up by saying that in a state of nature every man has a right to everything.

Accordingly the first and fundamental law of nature refers to the need to remove this fundamental insecurity; for my natural right to use my best efforts to preserve my life is not of much use to me if other men's exercise of their natural right leads them to try to kill me, or to act in other ways still disadvantageous to me, though less acutely so – the right of self-preservation is useless unless the means of successfully exercising the right are also given. It follows (and this is Hobbes's first law of nature) 'that every man, ought to endeavour peace, as far as he has hope of obtaining it' (*Leviathan* 85); this is the fundamental law of nature on which all the others depend.

The second law of nature is derived immediately from the first: 'that a man be willing, when others are so too, as far-forth, as for peace, and defence of himself he shall think necessary, to lay down this right to all things; and be contented with so much liberty against other men, as he would allow other men against himself' (*Leviathan* 85). Once again, the reference is to a necessary condition for the fulfilment of a requirement which has already been established. Peace is the necessary condition of any lasting and secure satisfaction of a man's desires; therefore a man must be prepared to do whatever is necessary to secure peace. But no man can achieve this end by his own efforts; his concessions will be of no value unless they are matched by other men (and are therefore not demanded by the law of nature except under that condition). Civil society, then, is possible only when a sufficiently large number of men inhabiting the same region have agreed to rid themselves of the intolerable evils of the state of nature in the only way in which this can be done, by the voluntary and reciprocal renunciation of part, at least, of the natural right which each of them originally possessed. In my attempts to satisfy my desires I will refrain from attacking you if you in return will refrain from attacking me. Now the object of such a voluntary renunciation is prudential, not moral; or more pedantically, it is not moral in any sense in which morality can be contrasted with or opposed to prudence – 'it is a voluntary act: and of the voluntary acts of every man, the object is some *good to himself*' (*Leviathan* 86). Nevertheless obligations arise from the renunciation which did not exist before it.

> Right is laid aside, either by simply renouncing it; or by transferring it to another . . . And when a man hath in either manner abandoned, or granted away his right; then he is said to be OBLIGED, or BOUND, not to hinder those, to whom such right is granted, or abandoned, from the benefit of it: and that he *ought*, and it is his DUTY, not to make void that voluntary act of his own: and that such hindrance is INJUSTICE, and INJURY as being *sine jure*; the right being before renounced, or transferred. (*Leviathan* 86)

In the state of nature a man had a right to anything which he deemed necessary to his preservation: nothing which he did with a view to preserving himself could be regarded as wrong or improper. This situation is so unsatisfactory for everyone that it is in a man's interest to give up, or to limit, this natural right, provided that others do so too; once this has been done, it follows that certain actions can henceforth be regarded as wrong or improper, simply because men have voluntarily given up the right to perform them.

The mutual transferring of right, required by the second law of nature, is called contract; but Hobbes is concerned principally with a special kind of contract, known as covenant, in which one or both of the parties may contract now to perform some action at a later time. A ready-money transaction, in which cash is handed over in return for the immediate provision of goods is a contract, not a covenant; but if I receive goods and undertake to pay for them in a year's time, I have made a covenant, and thereby promised, and the other party trusts me to perform. It is clear that the mutual transferring of right is a covenant of mutual trust in which both parties undertake to perform later and trust each other to do so; such a covenant, Hobbes says, is void (i.e. not binding) in a state of nature if there is any reasonable suspicion that the other party is not going to keep his part of it (provided that the suspicion arose only after the covenant was made – a previous suspicion should have deterred the suspicious party from making the covenant in the first place). A covenant to allow another to kill me if certain conditions are fulfilled, or not to defend my life in all circumstances, is also void:

no man can transfer, or lay down his right to save himself from death, wounds, and imprisonment, the avoiding whereof is the only end of laying down any right; and therefore the promise of not resisting force, in no covenant transferreth any right; nor is obliging. For though a man may covenant thus, *unless I do so, or so, kill me*; he cannot covenant thus, *unless I do so, or so, I will not resist you, when you come to kill me*. For man by nature chooseth the lesser evil, which is danger of death in resisting; rather than the greater, which is certain and present death in not resisting. (*Leviathan* 91–2)

Now since the mutual transference of right (i.e. covenanting on the principle of mutual trust) is a necessary condition for the establishment of the fundamental human need, peace and security, and since the making of covenants would be pointless if there were not a general expectation that they would be kept, Hobbes's third law of nature follows: *'that men perform their covenants made: without which, covenants are in vain, and but empty words; and the right of all men to all things remaining, we are still in the condition of war'* (*Leviathan* 93). This law is, in effect, the law which institutes and prescribes adherence to justice as a standard of conduct; until a covenant has been made, nothing can be unjust: when there is a covenant, not to perform one's part of it constitutes injustice, provided (and this is important) that there exists some power which will coerce the reluctant into keeping their covenants. The practice of justice in a state of nature can be dangerous to the just man; hence there is no obligation to the practice of justice until this danger has been removed.

Before the names of just, and unjust, can have place, there must be some coercive power, to compel men equally to the performance of their covenants, by the terror of some punishment, greater than the benefit they expect by the breach of their covenant; and to make good that propriety [sc. property], which by mutual contract men acquire, in recompense of the universal right they abandon; and such power there is none before the erection of a commonwealth. And this is also to be gathered out of the ordinary definition of justice in the Schools: for they say, that *justice is the constant will of giving to every man his own.* And therefore where there is no *own*, that is no propriety, there is no injustice; and where there is no coercive power erected, that is, where there is no commonwealth, there is no propriety; all men having right to all things: therefore where there is no commonwealth, there nothing is unjust. So that the nature of justice, consisteth in keeping of valid covenants: but the validity of covenants begins not but with the constitution of a civil power, sufficient to compel men to keep them: and then it is also that propriety begins. (*Leviathan* 94)

The other laws of nature enumerated by Hobbes mostly concern less important matters and I do not propose to enter into detailed discussion of them. He sums up the general tenor of the laws of nature by saying that they are 'contained in this one sentence, approved by all the world, *Do not that to another, which thou thinkest unreasonable to be done by another to thyself'* (*Leviathan* 177). What we do need to discuss is the status of the laws of nature in general. They seem at first sight to be no more than rules of prudence; that is, rules which an individual must follow if he is to achieve the conditions of peace and security necessary for the assured continuance of his life and for the rendering of that life reasonably pleasant and comfortable. He may have many obligations the fulfilling of which may seem to be burdensome to him, but there is no question for Hobbes of a rigid Kantian distinction between obligation and interest; for no obligation can be incurred by a man otherwise than through some voluntary act of his own (*Leviathan* 141), and the object of every voluntary act of a man is some good to himself (*Leviathan* 86). Hobbes does indeed strongly criticise those immoralists who agree that there is no reason why a man should not act unjustly, even in a commonwealth, if he thinks he can do so with advantage; but the strength of his criticism merely reflects the strength of his belief that, even though such unjust conduct can sometimes turn to a man's advantage, he can never, in advance, have any rational grounds for believing that it will. 'He therefore that breaketh his covenant, and consequently declareth that he thinks he may with reason do so, cannot be received into any society, that unite themselves for peace and defence, but by the error of them that receive him; nor when he is received, be retained in it, without seeing the danger of their error' (*Leviathan* 96); so either the man is destroyed by being thrust out of the society, or if he is not it is because of an error of judgment by his fellow-men which he could not reasonably have counted on. And this argument, which applies specifically to the law of nature which prescribes justice (i.e. the keeping of covenants) could presumably be generalised to apply to them all. The argument is not: it doesn't matter whether wickedness is successful or not, it's still wickedness and therefore to be avoided, but: even if wickedness is sometimes successful, no one can ever have sufficient grounds for believing that *his* will be successful to make it reasonable, on prudential considerations, for him to act wickedly – and where, one might ask, is the morality here?

(iv) THE ORIGINS OF MORAL OBLIGATION

There are two factors in Hobbes's account which make his purported move from purely individual considerations to morality one which is at least not obviously illegitimate. The first is that he is not simply trying to derive my moral obligation to keep my promises from the purely selfish consideration that I shall be worse off if I do not; if he were, there would be no reason to suppose that in pursuing my own interests I might not be seriously interfering with other men in the pursuance of theirs. The aim in question, however, is not my own interest in general, but the peace and security without which the successful pursuit of any of my interests is impossible; and this carries with it the corollary that in promoting my own peace and security I am inevitably promoting that of others, and that in acting with this very special kind of prudent concern for my own fundamental interests I am inevitably at the same time helping to promote the fundamental interests of all my actual or potential fellow-citizens. The aim of promoting peace and security is inevitably, in a sense, a social and other-regarding aim. My motive may be self-interest; but the end-product of the action must promote the desired end for everyone, not just for myself (it is presumably because of this fact that Hobbes has sometimes, rather misleadingly, been thought of as a kind of premature utilitarian). Kant, in a well-known passage in the *Critique of Practical Reason* (v 29), argued that man's desire for his own happiness or satisfaction could never be made the source of a universal principle of morality because the securing of one man's happiness may interfere with that of another's (in Kant's own example, Francis I and Charles V both want the same thing, but this does not mean that their desires are in harmony, for they both want the city of Milan, and obviously they cannot both have it). But Kant's objection, though in general sound, does not work against Hobbes, for the reasons I have given.

That Hobbes does attempt to make use of this identity of interest to derive moral principles from considerations of human nature in general and man's desires and needs in particular is clear from his general remarks about the laws of nature at the end of chapter xv of *Leviathan*. The science of these laws, he says, is the only true moral philosophy. For moral philosophy is the science of what is good and evil. But in the state of nature, as we have seen, there is no standard of good and evil save the manifold and differing appetites of the individual.

And therefore so long a man is in the condition of mere nature, which is a condition of war, as private appetite is the measure of good, and evil: and consequently all men agree on this, that peace is good, and therefore also the way, or means of peace, which, as I have shewed before, are *justice*, *gratitude*, *modesty*, *equity*, *mercy*, and the rest of the laws of nature, are good; that is to say; *moral virtues*; and their contrary *vices*, evil. Now the science of virtue and vice, is moral philosophy; and therefore the true doctrine of the laws of nature, is the true moral philosophy. But the writers of moral philosophy, although they acknowledge the same virtues and vices; yet not seeing wherein consisted their goodness; nor that they come to be praised, as the means of peaceable, sociable, and comfortable living, place them in a mediocrity of passions: as if not the cause, but the degree of daring, made fortitude; or not the cause, but the quantity of a gift, made liberality. (*Leviathan* 104)

In short, the moral virtues, the practice of which is prescribed by the laws of nature, are moral virtues (i.e. objectively good qualities) because the practice of them conduces to peace, which every man must acknowledge to be good.

Now it might be thought that there is a fallacy in the argument here analogous to the well-known one in J. S. Mill's *Utilitarianism* ('No reason can be given why the general happiness is desirable, except that each person, so far as he believes it to be attainable, desires his own happiness. This, however, being a fact, we have not only all the proof which the case admits of, but all which it is possible to require, that happiness is a good: that each person's happiness is a good to that person, and the general happiness, therefore, a good to the aggregate of all persons', Everyman ed., pp. 32–3). From the fact that my happiness is a good to me and your happiness is a good to you it obviously does not follow that our joint happiness is a good to both of us, if only because it may be that I cannot achieve my happiness without interfering with yours, and because the conjunction of two individual aims does not necessarily produce a single joint aim. Hobbes's position, however, is not open to this criticism, for although, in the abstract terms in which Mill's discussion takes place, in promoting my happiness I am not necessarily promoting yours, the peculiarity of Hobbes's position is that I cannot promote my fundamental good, namely security, without at the same time promoting yours; for no man, Hobbes has insisted, can achieve security for and by himself, but needs the co-operation of others just as they need his. A Hobbesian man, in agreeing that peace is good, does indeed agree that it is good for his fellows as well as for himself. It is true, of course, that the knowledge that peace is good for my fellows would not for Hobbes be a sufficient motive for my pursuing peace (the motive to action can come only from my knowing or believing that peace is good for me); the virtues of co-operation, nevertheless, are moral virtues for Hobbes, as they are for most of the more orthodox moral philosophers, even though the need for co-operation has its ultimate roots in self-interest.

The Hobbesian transition from egoistic or prudential considerations to moral ones may still, however, be regarded as unsatisfactory. To say to a man 'You ought to do that, because if you don't you jeopardise the security without which none of your desires can be fulfilled' is clearly not to make a moral judgment in any sense in which moral judgments are being distinguished from, as opposed to being assimilated to, prudential ones. Whatever the force of the 'ought', it is certainly not a moral 'ought', unless the word 'moral' is being used either as a synonym for 'prudential' or to stand for a sub-class of the prudential; and if it is being used in either of these ways the question 'How is the transition from prudence to morality being made?' does not arise – it is not being made at all, and does not need to be made. It might seem, on the other hand, that to say 'You ought to do that, because if you don't you jeopardise the security without which nobody's (or none of your fellow-citizens') desires can be achieved' is to make a moral judgment (at least it is an other-regarding, and so not simply a prudential, judgment); and if there is an inevitable identity of interest, why should this not serve to justify Hobbes's transition from interest to morality, as a transition from concern for oneself to concern for others?

It must be pointed out, however, that the 'morality' to which the supposed transition is being made is morality in what some would regard as a much attenuated sense of the term. There is no possibility on this view of a man having a moral motive for doing something as opposed to a prudential motive (this would be inconsistent with Hobbes's philosophy of action), still less of any moral obligation to do something contrary to his own interest; there is no suggestion in Hobbes of the argument 'Even if doing this won't do anything to help *you*, it will do much to help others, and therefore you ought to do it'. It has been argued recently by F. S. McNeilly in an important article 'Egoism in Hobbes' (*Philosophical Quarterly*, 16 (1966) 193–206) that a large part of Hobbes's doctrine of motivation in *Leviathan* (as opposed to the doctrines of *The Elements of Law*, *De Cive* and *De Corpore*) is non-egoistic; but while there is much to be said for this view, I do not think that there is any evidence to show that the doctrine was anti-egoistic, i.e. that it allowed for the possibility of a man voluntarily doing something which he thought to be contrary to his own interest. Aubrey has a story (*Brief Lives*, ed. Clark, 1 352) which suggests that Hobbes maintained his egoistic psychology even when he was not doing philosophy:

He was very charitable (*pro suo modulo*) to those that were true objects of his bounty. One time, I remember, goeing in the Strand, a poor and infirme old man craved his alms. He, beholding him with eies of pity and compassion, putt his hand in his pocket, and gave him 6d. Sayd a divine that stood by – 'Would you have donne this, if it had not been Christ's command?' – 'Yea', sayd he. – 'Why?' quoth the other. – 'Because', sayd he, 'I was in paine to consider the miserable condition of the old man; and now my almes, giving him some reliefe, doth also ease me.'

The second possible transition-point between self-interest and morality lies in the notion of covenant. A man may have a motive for making a covenant which consists solely in the advantage he expects to get out of the transaction; but having made it, he has an obligation to keep it which cannot consist simply in the fact (if it is a fact) that it will be to his advantage to do so – breaking a covenant is the essence of injustice, and this is not simply another word for self-interest. Hobbes does admittedly from time to time use words and expressions in novel and unusual ways ('law of nature' is a good example), and those who claim that all Hobbes's talk of obligation is intended by him to refer to nothing more than self-interest[4] might argue that 'justice' and 'injustice' are used by Hobbes in an attenuated sense which has little connection with the ordinary one. Hobbes, however, makes it clear that injustice in his sense (the 'not performance of covenant' (*Leviathan* 94)) is an injury to the person with whom the covenant was made (cp. *Leviathan* 97 'the injustice of an action, that is to say injury, supposeth an individual person injured; namely him, to whom the covenant was made'); and the insistence that not performing a covenant does an injury to the other party does not square well with the suggestion that, in Hobbes's view, the only objection to breaking a covenant is that it is against one's fundamental interest to do so. Since Hobbes believes that no man can bring himself to act in a way destructive of his life, it follows that no man can be reasonably expected so to act and therefore that no man has an obligation so to act. The fact, then, that in not performing a certain action I am injuring another man is not by itself sufficient to create for me an obligation, in the fullest sense, to perform it; the full obligation is created only if, in addition, it is safe for me so to act. Nevertheless even in a state of nature, when it may not be safe for a man to keep his covenants, the notion of obligation is not altogether excluded (this is the reason for the inclusion of the phrase 'in the fullest sense' in the last sentence).

The laws of nature oblige *in foro interno*; that is to say, they bind to a desire they should take place: but *in foro externo*; that is, to the putting them in act, not always. For he that should be modest, and tractable, and perform all he promises, in such time, and place, where no man else should do so, should but make himself a prey to others, and procure his own certain ruin, contrary to the ground of all laws of nature, which tend to nature's preservation. (*Leviathan* 103)

The notion of an obligation to desire something may strike us as odd; but a few sentences later Hobbes makes it clear that he thinks of the laws of nature as obliging us to 'an unfeigned and constant endeavour' (*Leviathan* 104) to act in accordance with them. The breaking of a promise is always essentially a warlike act and therefore to be avoided if possible; but if a man finds himself in a warlike situation in which it is not safe for him to perform what he has promised he may legitimately break the promise, as an act of self-defence in war, as it were. Nevertheless, this is a regrettable necessity, which is not merely to be regretted and lamented but to be avoided wherever there exists any possibility of so doing.

The importance of this reference to laws of nature obliging *in foro interno* is to make it clear that the obligation to obey them is not purely and simply a legal obligation (any more than it is purely and simply a matter of prudence, even if it is subtly and complicatedly a matter of prudence, to obey them). Hobbes had made this clear in a rather different way in the *De Cive*. 'Contracts', he there says (*EW* II 185) 'oblige us; laws tie us fast, being obliged'; and he explains this in a footnote as follows: '*To be obliged*, and *to be tied being obliged*, seems to some men to be one and the same thing; and that therefore here seems to be some distinction in words but none indeed. More clearly therefore I say thus: that a man is obliged by his contracts, that is, he ought to perform for his promise sake; but that the law ties him being obliged, that is to say, it compels him to make good his promise for fear of the punishment appointed by the law.' The mere fact of my having promised, or covenanted, to do something creates an obligation on me to do it, even though I cannot be held to the obligation unless I can perform it safely.

Also of interest in this context are some of Hobbes's remarks about equity, which is prescribed by the eleventh law of nature: 'if *a man be trusted to judge between man and man*, it is a precept of the law of nature, *that he deal equally between them*. For without that, the controversies of men cannot be determined but by war. He therefore that is partial in judgment, doth what in him lies, to deter men from the use of judges, and arbitrators; and consequently, against the fundamental law of nature' (*Leviathan* 101). In chapter 26 of *Leviathan*, where he is discussing various aspects of legislative and judicial procedure, he insists on the primacy of equity over precedent. If a legal decision, even though believed by the judge to be sound and fair, turns out to be inequitable, then it cannot bind a judge in any future case, for not even the most powerful judge (indeed, not even the sovereign) can properly

C

transgress a law of nature. 'Princes succeed one another; and one judge passeth, another cometh; nay, heaven and earth shall pass; but not one tittle of the law of nature shall pass; for it is the eternal law of God. Therefore all the sentences of precedent judges that have ever been, cannot altogether make a law contrary to natural equity' (*Leviathan* 181). The rhetorical language does, I think, express a genuine feeling of Hobbes that knowingly unfair treatment of accused persons in a court of law (and especially the punishment of people known to be innocent) is morally objectionable, not to say wicked. But is Hobbes justified, on his own principles, in this attitude? Is he justified in saying more than that inequitable treatment of offenders tends to promote war, not peace, and is therefore not in the general interest, nor in that of the partial judge himself?

Some commentators have held that Hobbes regards the will or command of God as that which, in the last analysis, gives authority to the laws of nature; and it is true that he frequently speaks of obedience to these laws as being commanded by God. Nevertheless, the reason why we ought to obey the laws of nature consists always, for Hobbes, in the fact that obedience to them leads to peace and disobedience to war; and no reference to God is required to show that peace is good and war evil – this has been established from the purely secular analysis of human desire and of the conditions necessary to satisfy it.[5] What Hobbes really feels strongly about, I suspect, is not the fact that God commands obedience to the laws of nature, but the peace and security which, in his view, cannot be achieved unless those laws are obeyed. And it is obvious that Hobbes, in recommending the pursuit, by the only available means, of the all-important peace and security, is not simply thinking of his own personal interests; as an individual he is certainly appalled by the prospect of the war-produced sufferings of mankind in general, not merely of his own, and impressed by the gain to mankind in general provided by the art, commerce, civilisation and culture which can exist only in conditions of peace. But does his philosophy entitle him to hold this position?

The answer is, I think, that Hobbes's philosophy, strictly

speaking, is neutral on the question of any motives that a man may have for desiring peace and security over and above the fundamental motive, namely the desire to secure the necessary conditions for the satisfaction of his own appetites and aversions, whatever they may be. Whatever Hobbes may actually say, his primary philosophical principles do not commit him to denying that a man might come to regard the good of others as part of his own good and thus to try to promote it without calculating on every occasion how much he personally would benefit from so doing. But although Hobbes can be interpreted as saying, on occasion at least, that men ought to keep their covenants for the general good, this does not imply that he is espousing a philosophical altruism inconsistent with his stated philosophy of action and its motives. A man cannot secure his own good without acting in a way that will in fact also secure the good of all his actual or potential fellow-citizens. Hobbes's philosophical conclusion is therefore quite independent of any egoistic psychology that he may originally have espoused or, at the time of writing *Leviathan*, have still been espousing. Even if a man can be interested in the welfare of others quite independently of any regard for his own, this by itself gives us no reason for challenging Hobbes's thesis that peace and security, and hence the conditions necessary for the establishment of peace and security, are the all-important ends of human conduct, and the basis on which moral and political philosophy must be constructed.

(v) THE LOGIC OF HOBBES'S ARGUMENT

The logic of Hobbes's argument, then, is clear: men have certain desires and aversions the secure fulfilment of any of which requires the establishment of conditions of peace and security; and this in turn requires men to make covenants of mutual trust with one another, the breaking of these covenants constituting injustice and moral wrongdoing. Now the latter part of this argument seems to present no difficulties of principle in respect of its logical structure, whatever problems might arise over some of the details. 'All promises ought to be kept; you have promised to do X; therefore you ought to do X' – nobody, surely, can fault the logic of this, assuming (and this, I think, can be fairly assumed) that the two 'oughts' have the same force. But those who have adopted the slogan 'No "ought" from an "is"' and who therefore are committed to the view that there must be something wrong with Hobbes's attempted derivation of moral rules from basic facts about human nature will perhaps claim that an error has been committed at an earlier stage of the argument: how can even the merely prudential 'ought' of 'Men ought to seek peace and security' be derived from a set of factual propositions about human nature, and in particular about human appetites and aversions?

To this claim it must be replied that the prudential 'ought' of the conclusion is legitimately derived, and that what makes the derivation legitimate is the special nature of the factual or 'ought'-propositions which function as the premisses of the inference. In the first place, there is no particular difficulty about the logical transition from wanting something to setting oneself to achieving or obtaining it. There are of course many situations in which a man wants something but does not try to obtain it (for example, because he wants something else even more and believes that he cannot have both the things he wants); but we are not entitled to conclude from this that there is a logical gap between wanting and trying to obtain that needs a logical bridge over it. What distinguishes the cases in which a man's wanting something leads him to try to obtain it from those in which it does not is not that there is some additional factor present in the former cases which is absent in the latter, but, on the contrary, that factors are present in the latter case which, as it were, defeat the presumption that is normally created by the use of the word 'want'. Someone may say to himself 'I would like an apple' and proceed without further ado to take one from a dish in front of him; there is here no logical gap between 'I would like' and 'I take'. But on another occasion someone might say 'I would like an apple but I don't think I shall have one because it might give me indigestion'; here the clause preceded by the word 'but' cancels the active effect of what has just been said – but the active effect or force is naturally understood unless it is explicitly cancelled in some such way as this. Hobbes's own account of appetites and aversions in terms of actual, though imperceptible, movements towards, or away from the desired or undesired object, is only an exaggerated version of this position. It is absurd, on any account, to say of someone, 'Yes, I know he wants X, but why should he attempt, or take the steps he thinks necessary, to obtain it?'; for if a man wants something, he does not need any additional motive or incentive to try to acquire it or to take any steps he thinks necessary to its acquisition. Hobbes has argued for the very general empirical thesis that security is a necessary condition for the attaining of any great number of a man's desires; therefore any man who has desires (and this means any man whatsoever) needs security and should attempt to secure it.

If a modern philosopher denies that the conjunction of 'Jones wants X' and 'Jones cannot have X without doing Y' logically entails, even when some proviso about the absence of any conflicting wants is added, that Jones ought (in a non-moral sense) to do X, there is, I suppose, no reason why he should not use the word 'entail' in this very strict way. What he cannot do is claim that 'Jones wants X' and 'Jones cannot have X without doing Y', taken together, provide no reason for Jones's doing Y; for Jones does not need, and it is stupid to ask for, any further reason. To insist on adding some such major premiss as 'Whenever a man wants anything, then he ought to do whatever is necessary to the obtaining of that thing' may help to relieve the logical conscience of the present-day anti-naturalist, but it does not in fact add anything substantial to the argument; for what it says has already been said in the more specific statements about Jones.

This defence of the logic of Hobbes's position may, however, serve to introduce a rather different kind of objection that may be made, not so much perhaps to his actual procedure as to his own view and description of that procedure. He thinks of himself, as we saw, as applying scientific and mathematical method to the study of man, and as achieving success in that study comparable to the successes of Galileo in physics and Harvey in physiology; and it is at least plausible, even if it is not in the end convincing, to suggest that a factual study of man's behaviour as an individual and in society could be successfully undertaken on scientific principles and by scientific methods. But Hobbes's philosophical study of man, it might be objected, is not primarily a factual one, even though some factual statements play an important part in his argument. He is trying to prove, not merely that men do inevitably and always behave in certain ways, but that in consequence of this and other general facts about human nature and about the world men ought to do certain things, and in particular that they ought to organise themselves into societies with certain special features and special rules of organisation. Scientific methods, it may be said, can establish the facts; but some other procedure is needed to establish the moral and political conclusions as to what men ought to do in the light of those facts. There was certainly no evidence available to Hobbes that scientific methods, whether contemporary or of earlier generations, had ever succeeded in establishing conclusions that went beyond the factual. But Hobbes, I suspect, would not have been impressed by this objection. The premisses which, when combined in a logical or quasi-mathematical way with scientifically ascertained facts yield evaluative or action-guiding conclusions, are propositions about what people want and how they can achieve what they want; and Hobbes, rightly or wrongly, believed that these propositions would be acceptable to any rational and intelligent man as soon as he reflected on, and understood, them.

III. HUME

(i) HUME'S NATURALISM

On the title-page of the *Treatise of Human Nature*, Hume describes the work as 'being an attempt to introduce the experimental method of reasoning into moral subjects'. The word 'moral' is here used in a wide sense in which it is contrasted with 'natural', and it is tempting to think of Hume as standing, or as trying to stand, in much the same relation to Newton, the chief practitioner of the 'experimental method', as Hobbes had done to (say) Galileo; both of them take current, or slightly earlier, scientific theory as their model, both think that the methods which have proved so fruitful in explaining the behaviour of inanimate matter can be applied, to a greater or lesser extent, to explaining, and otherwise treating of, the thoughts and activities of human beings. But although Hume's philosophical procedure is in many respects clearly modelled on what he takes to be Newtonian principles and method, the analogy with Hobbes can be misleading if it is pressed too far. For one thing, Hume at no time sets out to demonstrate his conclusions in the manner of a geometrical or strictly logical system, beginning with definitions and proceeding to regularly proved theorems. For another thing, Hume's 'naturalism' is human naturalism, so to speak; in spite of his admiration for, and attempted copying of, Newton, he does not try to connect moral phenomena with a systematic metaphysical account of the nature of the universe, but is simply applying a kind of scientific method to the study of the human mind. More important, Hume, unlike Hobbes, is not setting out (directly and ostensibly, at least) to draw from a scientific account of human nature practical conclusions as to how men ought to act. It is true that in the *Enquiry concerning the Principles of Morals* he says that 'the end of all moral speculations is to teach us our duty, and, by proper representations of the deformity of vice and beauty of virtue, beget correspondent habits, and engage us to avoid the one, and embrace the other' (*EM* 1 5, 172). But even if Hume's writing about morality has this ultimate purpose, the deduction of moral conclusions from factual premisses about human nature is not part of his philosophical programme. What he is attempting to do is, rather, to explain the observed facts of human nature by reducing them to as small a number of general principles as possible, and the intended analogy is with Newton's explanation of the behaviour of matter in terms of the laws of gravitation; the way in which, and the reasons for which, men do actually approve and disapprove morally of certain kinds of behaviour or character form part of the facts to be examined. It is important to notice that Hume's whole philosophy, and not just the part of it which has to do with morality, is concerned with the examination of human nature; he investigates the working of the human understanding or intellect, as well as that of human tastes, passions and sentiments. 'There is no question of importance, whose decision is not compriz'd in the science of man; and there is none, which can be decided with any certainty, before we become acquainted with that science. In pretending therefore to explain the principles of human nature, we in effect propose a compleat system of the sciences, built on a foundation almost entirely new, and the only one upon which they can stand with any security' (*T*, Introduction, xx). The science of man must be carried on by the methods which have brought success in the natural sciences, namely by experiment and observation; but in enquiring into the nature and causes of human thought and behaviour, the philosopher cannot make experiments with the same ease and usefulness as the natural philosopher, if only because men do not behave naturally when placed in artificially contrived situations. 'We must therefore glean up our experiments in this science from a cautious observation of human life, and take them as they appear in the common course of the world, by men's behaviour in company, in affairs, and in their pleasures. Where experiments of this kind are judiciously collected and compared, we may hope to establish on them a science, which will not be inferior in certainty, and will be much superior in utility to any other of human comprehension' (*T*, Introduction, xxiii).

(ii) MORAL SENTIMENTS

The essential foundation for Hume's moral philosophy is his insistence that men's ability and disposition to make moral judgments depend primarily on their passions and sentiments, not on their purely intellectual faculties. Moral approval and disapproval are sentiments, not deliverances of reason. Reason (by which Hume, like Hobbes, means reasoning or ratiocination) is limited to the discovery of matters of fact and relations between ideas (the latter corresponding closely to the modern philosopher's concept of analytic truth). In his negative criticism of rationalist ethics, Hume is thinking principally of writers such as Cudworth and Clarke, who had spoken of unchangeable relations of fitness and unfitness between things: relations which were perceived, not by sense-perception, but by reason or intellect alone. His main argument is simple. Reason is inert and cannot by itself produce action; but moral judgments do influence action; therefore moral judgments cannot be derived from reason. The discovery that the performance of a certain action will have certain effects (factual reasoning) or that you cannot act ungratefully to a man unless he has conferred some benefit on you (logical reasoning referring to relations between ideas) will influence an agent's decision only if he already has certain desires and feelings which may themselves combine with the rationally acquired knowledge to produce action. 'Reason, in a strict and philosophical sense, can have an influence on our conduct only after two ways: Either when it excites a passion by informing us of the existence of something which is a proper object of it; or when it discovers the connexion of causes and effects, so as to afford us means of exerting any passion' (T 459). Moral approbation inclines us to favour the performance, whether by ourselves or others, of the approved conduct or the acquisition and display of the approved quality of character, whereas if moral approbation had its source in reason alone, the knowledge or belief that an action or quality was morally good would produce no disposition in a man to perform that action or display that quality.

Much more important, however, than Hume's negative

criticism of the rationalists is his positive account of the nature and origin of moral judgments in terms of human sentiments[6] and passions. (That moral judgments are restricted to the field of human conduct and have no supernatural reference is stressed in a letter which Hume wrote to Francis Hutcheson on 16 March 1740: 'I wish from my Heart, I could avoid concluding, that since Morality, according to your Opinion as well as mine, is determin'd merely by Sentiment, it regards only human Nature and human Life . . . If Morality were determined by Reason, that is the same to all rational Beings: But nothing but Experience can assure us, that the Sentiments are the same. What Experience have we with regard to superior Beings? How can be ascribe to them any Sentiments at all?' (*The Letters of David Hume*, ed. J. Y. T. Greig (Oxford, 1932) I 40).) To say that moral approval and disapproval are sentiments, not deliverances of reason, is not by itself particularly informative; and the suggestion that there is a specifically moral sentiment, immediately recognisable as such, and independent of all other emotions and feelings is almost as obscurantist as the rationalist's picture of an independent rational faculty for making moral distinctions (although this has not prevented it becoming the basis of a whole modern type of ethics, namely what is called the emotive theory). Hume, however, makes no such suggestion. Our moral sentiments of approval and disapproval are, for him, closely connected with other, not specifically moral, feelings and emotions; and, in the *Treatise* at least, he regards it as one of his main tasks to exhibit the full extent and complexity of these connections (another being to explain the nature of the objectives towards which moral approval and disapproval are directed).

Hume's account of moral approval and disapproval is related by him to his general picture of the human mind as consisting of perceptions which are either ideas or impressions; to say that moral distinctions have their origin in sentiment, not reason, is to say that we distinguish between vice and virtue by means of our impressions, not our ideas. Impressions are of two kinds, original and secondary; the first are sense-impressions, while to the second class belong all the 'passions', i.e. feelings (excluding sensations of bodily pleasure and pain, which are original impressions), emotions and sentiments. Now the First Book of the *Treatise*, dealing with the operations of the understanding or intellect, made great use of the concept of the association of ideas as a unifying and explanatory principle. There is a tendency for one idea in the mind to give rise to another when there is between them a relation of resemblance, or contiguity, or causation. The importance which Hume attached to this principle can be seen from his reference to it in the *Abstract* of the *Treatise*, which purported to be a reader's summary, but was in fact written by Hume himself: 'Through this whole book there are great pretensions to new discoveries in philosophy; but if anything can entitle the author to so glorious a name as that of an "inventor", it is the use he makes of the principle of the association of ideas, which enters into most of his philosophy' (p. 198 of Hendel's edition of the *Enquiry concerning Human Understanding*). Hume goes on to say that the three principles according to which ideas are associated, namely contiguity, resemblance and causation, are 'the only links that bind the parts of the universe together or connect us with any person or object exterior to ourselves. For as it is by means of thought only that anything operates upon our passions, and as these are the only ties of our thoughts, they are really *to us* the cement of the universe, and all the operations of the mind must, in a great measure, depend on them' (ibid.).

In Book II of the *Treatise* Hume introduces the analogous principle of the association of impressions. Here, however, the associative principle is resemblance only: 'All resembling impressions are connected together, and no sooner one arises than the rest immediately follow. Grief and disappointment give rise to anger, anger to envy, envy to malice, and malice to grief again, till the whole circle be compleated. In like manner our temper, when elevated with joy, naturally throws itself into love, generosity, pity, courage, pride, and the other resembling affections' (*T* II i iv 283). The two kinds of association frequently work simultaneously, and Hume makes great use of this fact in the *Treatise* to explain the detailed phenomena of the passions. It is not necessary for us to examine the whole of this psychology of the emotions, much of which has only a tenuous connection with Hume's moral philosophy. It is worth drawing attention, however, to a fairly constant feature of Hume's procedure in making these explanations, because it relates to his adherence to the experimental method of argument and demonstration. He constantly begins with what may fairly be called an *a priori* account of the situation, i.e. of the way in which a particular passion or combination of passions may be originated by the joint operation of the principles of association of ideas and of impressions, and then proceeds to confirm his *a priori* thesis 'experimentally'; i.e. by applying it to specific examples of human feeling and behaviour and showing how it is borne out by the facts of human nature. Take, for example, his account of the related passions of love, hate, pride and humility. The theoretical or *a priori* account asserts the existence of overlapping sets of relations, some primarily of ideas, the others primarily of impressions. Pride and humility are related by association of ideas, in that their object is the proud or humble man himself: love and hatred are similarly related, in that they are directed to some object other than the loving or hating man. Pride and love, on the other hand, are related by association of impressions, in that they are both agreeable passions: humility and hatred are similarly related, because they are both disagreeable, or 'uneasy', passions. 'I say then', Hume concludes (*T* II II ii 333), 'that nothing can produce any of these passions without bearing it a double relation, viz. of ideas to the object of the passion, and of sensation to the passion itself.' Eight systematic 'experiments' designed to prove this thesis are then described. One such experiment, to which I may refer by way of example, is designed to prove that the double relation of impressions and ideas is necessary for the existence of the relevant passion by showing that the association of impressions is not by itself enough to do so: if I am travelling with a companion through a country to which we are both strangers, I may be put into a good humour with myself and with my fellow-traveller by the beauty of the scenery, the smoothness of the roads and the comfort of the inns, but, as long as we assume that the country has no special relationship to either of us, the emotions of pride and love can never be produced in this way.

34

(iii) SYMPATHY

Of crucial importance for Hume's account of the nature of moral judgment is his use of the concept of sympathy. By this he means not a specific feeling or emotion of compassion but a general tendency to feel whatever emotions or passions we observe in others. The idea of an emotion (i.e. the perception by one man that another man is feeling it) is turned into the corresponding impression; we tend to feel happy or angry, for example, when we observe others feeling happy or angry. 'A chearful countenance infuses a sensible complacency and serenity into my mind; as an angry or sorrowful one throws a sudden damp upon me. Hatred, resentment, esteem, love, courage, mirth and melancholy; all these passions I feel more from communication than from my own natural temper and disposition' (T II I xi 317). In the *Treatise* Hume gives a somewhat elaborate account of the way in which this sympathy arises. What he calls 'the idea, or rather impression of ourselves' (ibid.) is, he says, always present with us; and because of the pervasive fact of consciousness this conception of ourselves is as lively and vivid as any can be. But by the laws of association, anything related to us, whether by causation, resemblance or contiguity, will present itself to our mind with the same vividness. Human beings are very much alike and exhibit broadly similar patterns of emotional behaviour; frequently then, when I observe the feelings and emotions of others I know that I have often in the past felt as they do in analogous situations and shall do so again in the future (resemblance), and there are special reasons for the liveliness and vividness of my ideas when the people of whose feelings I am aware are close at hand (contiguity) or blood relations (causation). 'All these relations, when united together, convey the impression or consciousness of our own person to the idea of the sentiments or passions of others, and makes us conceive them in the strongest and most lively manner' (T II I xi 318). Now it is part of Hume's general theory of impressions and ideas that they differ only in degree of force and vivacity, and that consequently 'the lively idea of any object always approaches its impression'. So the idea of another's passion, made lively by its association with my impression of myself, is liable to turn into an impression of the passion, i.e. into the passion itself.

When he came to write the *Enquiry*, Hume treated the existence of sympathy (or humanity, as he now preferred to call it) as a basic and unexplained fact. 'It is needless to push our researches so far as to ask, why we have humanity or a fellow-feeling with others. It is sufficient that this is experienced to be a principle in human nature. We must stop somewhere in our examination of causes; and there are, in every science, some general principles beyond which we cannot hope to find any principle more general' (*EM* v ii 47 n1, 219 n1). An appendix to the *Treatise* makes it clear that Hume had soon become thoroughly dissatisfied with his whole account of personal identity, without having anything better to put in its place. The uneasy phrase already quoted 'the idea, or rather impression of ourselves' indicates one source of difficulty. Which is it to be? If idea, then his insistence that ideas differ from impressions only in being less lively and vivid makes it impossible for him to say, as his explanation of the origin of sympathy requires him to say, that our conception (to use his tactfully neutral word) of ourselves is an exceptionally vivid one. And whether it is idea or impression, almost everything that he says about personal identity in Book 1 of the *Treatise* would have to be abandoned; for he there insists that there can be no impression of the self, and consequently no idea of it either. But the causal explanation of sympathy, we may agree with Hume, is not an essential feature of a philosophical account of the situation. If it is a fact that men can feel the joys and misfortunes of others, and so come to have a regard for the welfare of others which is not simply a function of self-interest, then it is an important fact for moral philosophy, and especially for a moral philosophy, like Hume's, which is based on an account of the nature of man. (This is only one of a number of respects in which the optimistic attitude of the *Treatise* did not long survive its publication; and the two *Enquiries* are much more modest in their claims.)

Given that there exists in man this fundamental principle of sympathy, what is its relation to morality? In broad outline, Hume's answer is this. We feel moral approval for a quality according as it is either useful or agreeable either to its possessor or to others (and correspondingly with moral disapproval, 'harmful' and 'disagreeable' being substituted for 'useful' and 'agreeable'); moral approval and disapproval being, respectively, pleasant and unpleasant sentiments or feelings which we experience when we contemplate the qualitites in question as disinterested spectators. And we feel pleased (in this special way of feeling pleased that constitutes moral approbation) at the idea of pleasure being caused to others than ourselves or at the idea of the interests of others being furthered because of our propensity to sympathise with the happiness of others, i.e. to feel pleased when they feel pleased, and in general to rejoice in their well-being: and we feel displeased (in the special way of feeling displeased that constitutes moral disapprobation) at the idea of displeasure or harm being caused to others because of our propensity to sympathise with the displeasure or evil condition of others, i.e. to feel displeased when they are displeased and in general to feel unhappy at their unhappiness or disadvantage.

(iv) HUME'S DEFENCE OF HIS MORAL PHILOSOPHY

We now have to add some detail to this broad outline and to examine the manner in which (in conformity with his 'Newtonian' principles) Hume defends his thesis. The first point to be clear about is that for Hume moral judgments are about moral qualities or about actions considered as signs of such qualities, and not about actions in the abstract. ''Tis evident, that when we praise any actions, we regard only the motives that produced them, and consider the actions as signs or indications of certain principles in the mind and temper. The external performance has no merit' (T III II i 477). The moral appropriateness or inappropriateness of actions is a function of the moral appropriateness or inappropriateness of motives; if we blame someone for doing a wrong action (e.g. hurting someone's feelings or breaking a promise), then we are strictly blaming him for not being influenced by the proper motive. It follows, Hume maintains, 'that no action can be virtuous, or morally good, unless there be in human nature some motive to produce it, distinct from the sense of its morality' (ibid. 479). Before we can praise a man for his conduct, we require to know, not merely that what he has done is in accordance with rules which prescribe external conduct (for he may have kept a promise, or helped someone in distress, for purely self-interested reasons, in which case he deserves no moral praise), but also that he did what he did from a good, virtuous motive. And this means that he must have done what he did because he believed that it was his duty to do it. If he was right in believing this, there must have been something about the action which made it his duty to perform it; and this 'something' must have been connected with the motive from which acts, in such circumstances, ought to be performed. We blame a father for neglecting his child, Hume thinks, because such neglect displays a lack of that natural affection which is the duty of every parent.

But, one may ask, is 'natural affection' here a feeling the presence of which in a man causes him to care for his children, or is it rather the disposition to look after one's children without requiring a further motive for so doing? If it is the former, then do we really blame a man for not having a specific feeling? And even if we do, this is certainly not the whole story as far as blame for neglect is concerned; a man who lacks this feeling but who looks after his children properly for some other reason is not blameworthy in exactly the same way and for the same reasons as the man who lacks the feeling and who consequently neglects his children. We may feel that the first man lacks an important human quality; but he is at least performing the right actions, even if his motive for performing them is not a praiseworthy one. But if it is the latter, i.e. if affection is not a mere feeling but a disposition to act, then what we blame a man for, according to Hume, is that he *needs* an ulterior motive to make him look after his children properly. This may be right, but it does not follow that a virtuous motive is required to render an action virtuous; for the affectionate man who does look after his children does not have to have a motive for looking after them at all, in the sense of the word 'motive' that Hume's argument requires. The trouble is that he is using the word 'motive' to cover at least two different concepts, that of cause and that of reason. He sometimes thinks of a motive as a cause, i.e. as an independently existing event which functions as the cause of another independently existing event, namely the action in question (in this sense, a feeling of fear causes a man to run away). But he sometimes thinks of a motive as a reason, i.e. as a factor which a man can rationally take account of when he is engaged in deliberation whether he should perform a certain action or not (not necessarily, of course, in a moral sense of the word 'should'); and the point about the naturally affectionate man is that his behaviour does not need a reason of this kind at all, simply because he does not ask himself 'Why should I behave like this?' and does not need to ask himself this. Of course, a philosopher with a completely egoistic psychology of action would have to explain that the naturally affectionate man is in some way thinking of his own pleasure or interest when he behaves affectionately; but Hume is not a psychological egoist, and does not need to indulge in absurdities of this kind.

The important point for our purpose is that Hume, whether for good reasons or for bad, considers himself obliged to explain how it is that men can have a reason for acting with a view to the pleasure or interests of others in order to explain how it is that moral approval can consist in a sentiment of pleasure at such action, or rather at the virtuous qualities which are the source of such action. Although, as has been indicated, the concept of sympathy plays an important part in this explanation, the discussion takes two different forms, according as the virtues in question are natural or artificial. The artificial virtues are those which are prescribed by rules of justice. 'The only difference betwixt the natural virtues and justice lies in this, that the good, which results from the former, arises from every single act, and is the object of some natural passion: Whereas a single act of justice, consider'd in itself, may often be contrary to the public good; and 'tis only the concurrence of mankind, in a general scheme or system of action, which is advantageous' (*T* III III i 579). To act generously is *eo ipso* to promote the good of some other human being or beings: but for a man to act justly on one particular occasion need not be in anyone's interest at all. Yet men do approve of justice and

D

disapprove of injustice and Hume, in accordance with his general theory, has to show that this is due to the existence of *some* connection between the practice of justice and the general interest of other men, even though the connection is not as simple as it is with a natural virtue like generosity.

(v) TWO QUESTIONS ABOUT JUSTICE

Hume asks himself two questions about justice: (i) How do rules of justice come to be established? and (ii) Why do men approve morally of obedience to these rules and disapprove of their neglect?

(i) Man, unlike many animals, can survive in the conditions of nature only if he is united to fairly large numbers of his fellow-men in some form of society. But men's natural propensity to favour their own interests and those of their nearest kin and acquaintance tends to militate against the necessary social cohesion; and this is especially inconvenient in respect of a man's enjoyment of his material possessions, which others may be tempted to take from him for their own use, and the replenishment of which may be rendered difficult by natural scarcity. But since man's natural affections, even when mediated by sympathy, can do nothing to improve this situation, some form of contrivance is needed: 'The remedy, then, is not deriv'd from nature, but from *artifice*; or more properly speaking, nature provides a remedy in the judgment and understanding, for what is irregular and incommodious in the affections' (*T* III II ii 489). Men enter into a convention whereby they agree to abstain from interference with one another's property, recognising that this agreed mutual non-interference will be in their general interest. Hume is at pains to point out that this convention is not a promise; for he thinks that the obligation to keep promises is itself derivable from one of the human conventions concerning justice and cannot itself therefore be used to explain the origin of justice. There is no formality about it: a number of individuals recognise simultaneously that their interests will be served by placing certain limitations on their freedom of behaviour, and each in practice places these limitations on his own conduct, on the understanding that the others will do the same. Hume likens this convention which is not yet a promise to a situation in which two men pull the oars of a boat in agreement and, more importantly, to the conventions from which a natural language takes its origin. Men do certain things in concert by agreement, even though they do not sit down and conclude a formal agreement to do them.

Once the decision to have some rules limiting freedom has been taken, questions of detail may arise as to the form which the specific rules should take; but it is the first general convention that establishes the concepts of justice and injustice, and those of property, right, and obligation. Hume has an interesting comment at this point on the use many philosophers have made of the concept of a state of nature, a pre-social condition of man. He argues that it is quite impossible for men to have existed for any length of time in such a condition; the basic rule of justice is a very simple one and it is unthinkable that men should put up with the unstable conditions of an existence in which rules of property and justice are unheard of when they could so easily rid themselves of the instability and all its consequent evils. Nevertheless, Hume thinks, the concept of the state of nature may be legitimately used by philosophers as long as it is regarded as a philosophical fiction: not as a quasi-historical account of an actual situation, but as a theoretical account of the situation in which men would find themselves if they were not capable of thinking as well as of feeling. Natural philosophers may treat a single motion as if it were compounded of two different motions: moral philosophers, equally, may treat actual human behaviour as if it were compounded of two distinct factors, the contributions, respectively, of the feelings and the intellect, even though it is in actual fact one uncompounded piece of behaviour.

(ii) So far we have explained what Hume calls the 'natural obligation' to justice: Hume is saying that men's motive for setting up rules of justice is a kind of self-interest. They are obliged (but not, as far as the present argument has shown, morally obliged or under a moral obligation) to set up such rules because, if they do not, their interests will be seriously impaired.

But how does moral obligation become attached to justice? The larger a society becomes, the weaker becomes the influence of interest as a motive for obeying the rules of justice; for one thing, it is less likely that one breach of the rules will cause the collapse of the whole system. It is sympathy, as we should expect, that mediates the transition from self-interest to morality. I object to another man's breach of a rule of justice, even where it does not injure me, through sympathy at the injury done to the man who is unjustly treated, even if he is neither relative, friend, nor acquaintance of mine. Moreover, I extend my disapproval even towards my own unjust actions, however greatly to my own advantage those actions may have been. 'The *general rule* reaches beyond those instances, from which it arose; while at the same time we naturally *sympathize* with others in the sentiments they entertain of us. *Thus self-interest is the original motive to the establishment of justice: but a* sympathy *with public interest is the source of the* moral approbation, *which attends that virtue*' (T III II iii 499–500).

Hume's general conclusion about the artificial virtues is this: whether we consider the rules of justice in the strict sense, the obligation to political allegiance, the laws governing conduct between nations, or the rules prescribing chastity and modesty of behaviour, we are faced with a set of human contrivances designed to promote the interest of society and of the human beings who compose it. Our sentiments of approval and disapproval which are aroused by the contemplation of the mental qualities which motivate obedience or disobedience to these rules have their origin in the fact that, as a result of sympathy, we have a concern for the general interest of society which obedience to the rules promotes and which is threatened by disobedience; 'sympathy is the source of the esteem, which we pay to the artificial virtues' (T III III i 577).

(vi) THE NATURAL VIRTUES

There is a strong presumption, Hume thinks, that the same is true of the natural virtues; and this is borne out by the fact that we find that most of the qualities which we naturally and directly approve of do tend to promote the good of mankind and that most of those which we naturally and directly disapprove of tend to the contrary end. In other words, there is once again a general theory which is tested by reference to the detailed facts of human experience and behaviour. The attempt at a detailed confirmation of the theory is perhaps clearer in the *Enquiry* than in the *Treatise*, since in the later work Hume not only discusses those virtues which most plausibly support his thesis but also considers some possible objections. Generosity, for example, might seem to be a virtue our approval of which strongly supports Hume's case. But is generosity always a virtue? Cannot indiscriminate giving sometimes be an object of moral disapproval? Hume's answer is that it can, but that where we disapprove of an act of generosity our disapproval still rests on the principle of the general interest; i.e. we disapprove of it only when, because of special circumstances, it is likely to do more harm than good.

In all determinations of morality, this circumstance of public utility is ever principally in view; and wherever disputes arise, either in philosophy or common life, concerning the bounds of duty, the question cannot, by any means, be decided with greater certainty than by ascertaining, on any side, the true interests of mankind. If any false opinion, embraced from appearances, has been found to prevail, as soon as further experience and sound reasoning have given us juster notions of human affairs, we retract out first sentiment and adjust anew the boundaries of moral good and evil. (*EM* ii ii 12–13, 180)

If we do not stop to think, we naturally praise the generosity which leads a man to give alms to beggars, as contributing to the relief of distress; 'but when we observe the encouragement thence arising to idleness and debauchery, we regard that species of charity rather as a weakness than a virtue' (ibid.).

There are those who include in their list of virtues qualities which have no tendency to promote human welfare; but for this very reason their claims can be seen to be mistaken. 'Celibacy, fasting, penance, mortification, self-denial, humility, silence, solitude, and the whole train of monkish virtues – for what reason are they everywhere rejected by men of sense but because they serve to no manner of purpose; neither advance a man's fortune in the world, nor render him a more valuable member of society;

neither qualify him for the entertainment of company, nor increase his power of self-enjoyment' (*EM* IX i 91, 270).

I have so far been concentrating on one of Hume's four groups of virtuous qualities, those which we approve because they are useful to others. The other three groups can be dealt with more briefly. First, we approve of some qualities because they are useful, not necessarily or only to others, but to their possessor: industry, patience, temperance and frugality, for example. Some of these may be beneficial to society as a whole, but entirely apart from this consideration we approve of them (and disapprove of such qualities as prodigality and laziness) for their good or bad effects on their possessor. Secondly, we approve of some qualities because they are immediately agreeable (though not necessarily useful) to others; e.g. wit and eloquence. Thirdly and finally, we approve of some qualities because they are immediately agreeable to their possessor; e.g. good humour. With all these types of quality, the operation of the principle of sympathy or humanity is the important factor in producing our approval of them.

Hume's argument for his general thesis seems to beg the question. If the thesis to be proved is that all qualities which are genuinely virtuous promote human well-being, then a counterclaim that qualities *X*, *Y* and *Z* are virtues cannot be refuted by pointing out that they do not promote human well-being. Nor will it suffice to say, rhetorically, that they are 'everywhere rejected by men of sense'; a philosopher must be prepared to prove that his opponents are not men of sense, not simply assert it. Moreover, his thesis is not that most men, being sensible, value human qualities to the extent that they are agreeable or useful to their possessor or to others, even if a few men, being less sensible, have different principles of valuation: his thesis is that all men, because of the fundamental constitution of human nature, value human qualities in this way. Accordingly, apparent cases of people who do not accept Hume's account of moral approval and disapproval and who make what purport to be moral judgments on a different basis constitute a serious *prima facie* objection to Hume's position, and require a less cursory treatment. However, he is entitled to a rather better defence of his thesis than the one which he actually employs. He is entitled to argue that, if a human quality is generally good or bad, as the case may be, and thus virtuous or vicious, there must be something about it which makes it good or bad (goodness and badness, virtue and vice, are consequential qualitites); and he could then go on to ask someone who claimed that self-denial (say) was a virtue what there was about self-denial that made it a virtue or (and this comes to the same thing) what reasons he had for asserting that it was a good quality. Now to reply that self-denial is a virtue because its exercise can produce consequences that are pleasant or valuable to the agent or to others would, of course, play into Hume's hands, even if the asserted usefulness belonged to a man's future existence in the next world rather than to his present existence in this one; Hume has no need to deny that the occasional restraint of one's natural appetites can be beneficial to oneself or to others. What he must deny is that such restraint can be good in itself, i.e. that a value attaches to self-denial irrespective of any good or pleasant consequences it may bring to anyone. He is not even committed to arguing that the beneficial effects of the exercise of a moral virtue must be direct or immediate: he could, if he wished, argue that self-denial is, on occasions, good because it helps to train or develop a man's character, and that a man with a character developed in this way will lead a more agreeable or a more useful life (or both) than one with a character not so developed. Indeed Hume could if he wished incorporate a whole ethics of self-realisation within his own position, provided that the end or achievement of self-realisation, however that is to be defined, could be regarded as contributing to human well-being (and what self-realisationist philosopher would not regard it in this light?). Hume is not restricted to any narrowly utilitarian view of morality; for him 'utility' means usefulness for any desired end or purpose, not just usefulness for the purpose of producing pleasure and reducing or preventing pain.

(vii) HUME ON 'IS' AND 'OUGHT'

How far is Hume's account of moral judgments open to the objections brought (by such modern philosophers as Moore and

Hare) against naturalism in ethics on the score of logical confusion; does he make an illegitimate jump from statements of fact about human nature to judgments of morality? Hume is often represented, and with some justice, as being one of the first philosophers to draw attention to logical confusions of this kind. In a famous passage in the *Treatise* (*T* III I i 469) he complains that compilers of moral systems who begin with an account of the existence of God or of some aspect of human affairs proceed, without explanation, to pass from propositions containing the words 'is' and 'is not' to propositions with 'ought' and 'ought not'. 'This change is imperceptible; but is, however, of the last consequence. For as this *ought*, or *ought not*, expresses some new relation or affirmation, 'tis necessary that it shou'd be observ'd and explain'd; and at the same time that a reason should be given, for what seems altogether inconceivable, how this new relation can be a deduction from others, which are entirely different from it.' It is a matter of some interest to speculate what Hume, if he had read Hobbes's *Leviathan* carefully (and there is no evidence to suggest that he did) would have thought of that transition from an 'is' to an 'ought'. Hobbes certainly did 'observe and explain' the 'ought' and could hardly have been included in Hume's slighting reference to 'all the vulgar systems of morality' (*T* 470) which he thinks can be subverted by noticing the importance of the 'is'–'ought' distinction. Hume presumably[7] wishes to suggest, not merely that no philosophical system has yet shown how 'ought'-propositions can be deduced from 'is'-propositions, but also that no such deduction is possible. However, he produces no argument to show that it is impossible, and cannot therefore be regarded as a serious anti-naturalist, in the rather misleading sense which that term has now come to have. Indeed, the quoted passage follows immediately on a section of argument in which Hume has been stressing his point that moral distinctions are derived from sentiment, not from reason; morality is for Hume, as much as it is for any modern 'naturalist', rooted in the facts of human nature, even if 'ought'-judgments cannot be deduced, or derived in any other straightforward logical manner, from 'is'-judgments. He sometimes speaks, indeed, as if he intends to solve the logical problem by

46

denying the contrast between questions of fact and questions of morality altogether, and consequently removing the appearance of a logical gap which needs somehow or other to be bridged; this occurs when he asserts that moral judgments simply are factual judgments, even though they refer to facts about the mind or sentiment of the person who is making the judgment, not about the action or quality that is being judged. 'When you pronounce any action or character to be vicious, you mean nothing, but that from the constitution of your nature, you have a feeling or sentiment of blame from the contemplation of it. Vice and virtue, therefore, may be compar'd to sounds, colours, heat and cold, which, according to modern philosophy, are not qualities in objects, but perceptions in the mind' (*T* III 1 i 469). In a letter to Hutcheson from which I have already quoted, Hume expressed concern that this might be 'laid a little too strong' (*Letters*, ed. Greig, II 39–40); but it is clear from the context that he is doubting the prudence of saying such a thing publicly more than he is doubting its truth.

But if Hume is really asserting an identity of meaning between (i) 'On contemplating in a disinterested way your action and the quality of character it evinced, I experience a specifically moral feeling of disapproval', (ii) 'Your action exhibited a vicious quality of character' and (iii) 'You ought not to have done what you did', is he not avoiding one logical difficulty at the expense of involving himself in another at least as serious? He would seem to be 'solving' the problem, which he has after all explicitly recognised as a problem, of how to move logically from an 'is' to an 'ought' by asserting, or at least implying, that the 'ought' is really a kind of 'is'. It is true that his language can be interpreted as asserting something rather less than a strict identity of meaning: Hume was not a pedant, and 'When you pronounce —— you mean nothing but ——' may simply be his somewhat rhetorical way of saying that the only *fact* that is being asserted when you pronounce an action or character to be vicious is the fact that from the constitution of your nature you have a feeling or sentiment of blame from the contemplation of it (leaving open the possibility that the 'ought'-utterance has some force which the sentiment-stating utterance does not, even though the factual content is the same). It is true also that his language is sometimes less strong than in the passage I have quoted, and on occasions clearly implies some kind of connection only rather than an identity between the making of a moral judgment and the assertion that the maker of it experiences a certain feeling (cp. *T* III II v 517: 'When any action, or quality of the mind pleases us *after a certain manner*, we say it is virtuous; and when the neglect, or non-performance of it, displeases us *after a like manner*, we say that we lie under an obligation to perform it'). What Hume is saying here is that the existence of a certain feeling or sentiment is a sufficient (and perhaps also a necessary) condition for our asserting the existence (and apparently therefore of the existence itself) of an obligation; and whether Hume had seen the implications of the distinction or not, it is clearly possible to hold a view of this latter kind without asserting an actual identity between the obligation-judgment and the judgment asserting the existence of the sentiment. But Hume is here in a dilemma the full extent of which he does not seem to have recognised. If he adopts the weaker version of the thesis, namely that propositions such as 'You ought not to have done that' or 'You acted viciously in doing that' are asserted whenever the speaker has a certain kind of feeling or sentiment brought about by disinterested contemplation of the action, the question of the logical relationship between the 'ought'-proposition (or other moral proposition) and the sentiment-asserting proposition has not been answered: in particular, is it the case that the former is true if and only if the latter is true, and if it is the case, how can it be shown to be so? All that Hume has shown is that under certain conditions our having a feeling of disapproval leads us to say that the action is vicious or ought not to have been performed; but is it not possible to say to someone 'You have this feeling of disapproval, but is the action in respect of which you have the feeling really vicious?' (this is not to ask him if he really has the feeling, but, roughly, to ask him whether the feeling he has is an appropriate one).

If, on the other hand, Hume, when pressed, preferred to adopt the stronger form of the thesis, his difficulty would be a different one. We normally take such utterances as 'You ought not to have done that' or 'Your action was wrong and vicious' as having a blaming or criticising force, not just a fact-stating one (if indeed they have a fact-stating force at all); but if they are identical in meaning with 'I have a feeling of disapproval when I contemplate your action disinterestedly', where does this force have its origin? How does what purports to be a statement about my feelings come to be interpreted as a criticism of your action? It is true, of course, that such utterances as 'I disapprove of what you have done' can have a critical force; but they have this force to the extent that they are not simply (or in some cases perhaps not at all) autobiographical statements about the feelings or attitudes of the speaker. (Just as 'I don't like that colour', uttered while I am helping to choose some curtain material, is not simply a statement about my likes and dislikes but is also a suggestion that the material in question should be rejected.) The difficulty is that Hume's philosophical theory seems to require him to interpret 'I disapprove of your action' strictly as an assertion of the state of the speaker's own moral feelings or sentiments (if not, what becomes of his attempt to show that the making of moral judgments is rooted in the conditions of human nature?); and 'You ought not to have done that' is quite clearly not an assertion of my own moral feelings or sentiments, even if it is perhaps true that I would not have uttered it if I had not had the feeling or sentiment.

Although some of Hume's more incautious statements give the impression that he makes no distinction between a man's feeling disapproval and the actual existence (as opposed to the assertion of, or belief in) the existence of a corresponding obligation, the element of subjectivity involved in his views should not be exaggerated. He is at pains to distinguish purely individual reactions to a situation from the moral sentiment of approbation or disapprobation which results from a disinterested survey and contemplation.

When a man denominates another his *enemy*, his *rival*, his *antagonist*, his *adversary*, he is understood to speak the language of self-love and to express sentiments peculiar to himself and arising from his particular circumstances and situation. But when he bestows on any man the

49

epithets of *vicious* or *odious* or *depraved*, he then speaks another language and expresses sentiments in which he expects all his audience to concur with him. He must here, therefore, depart from his private and particular situation and must choose a point of view common to him with others: he must move some universal principle of the human frame and touch a string to which all mankind have an accord and symphony. (*EM* ix i 93, 272)

Hume believes that most people's moral judgments about any given state of affairs, provided that they are genuine moral judgments, not partial and biased opinions masquerading as such, will be in agreement; and although he does not pay much attention to the phenomenon of moral disagreement, he would presumably attribute much of it, at least, to disagreement as to the tendency of certain kinds of action or character to contribute to the public welfare or the well-being of the individual concerned. The fact that his is an 'agent-ethics' rather than an 'act-ethics' perhaps makes it less urgent for him to consider how moral disagreements are, or can be, resolved. No doubt his willingness to play down disagreement may spring in part from the assumption that, human nature being basically the same everywhere, all unbiased and knowledgeable men would be in broad agreement about matters of morality and taste. Like many others who have written about a fundamental, unchanging 'human nature', Hume takes his notion of it largely from an examination of the thoughts, practices and sentiments of the educated and cultured eighteenth-century European. He is aware, of course, that other kinds of human being have thought and felt differently, and that many have valued, and still value qualitities that a good Humean would condemn, and condemn qualities that he would value. Most of these differences, however, would have been dismissed by Hume as aberrations: primitive people, for example, or people under the influence of superstition, might have their sense of values perverted, but the perversion presumably takes the form of ignorance of facts or inability to make correct inferences, and the fact that such people disagree with what Hume regards as a correct morality is no evidence that it is incorrect. But it is also easier to find agreement on the qualities of character which are in general useful or agreeable than on such questions as 'What ought a man to do in such-and-such a situation?'. For one difficulty with questions of this kind is that a man may well display praiseworthy and admirable qualities in performing any of a quite considerable number of actions in any one given situation. As long as we confine our attention to the question 'Were the qualitities he displayed praiseworthy ones?' the answer may be straightforward and unlikely to be disputed: but if we ask: 'Did he do the right, i.e. the best, thing in that situation?' the question becomes much more complex and is more likely to receive diverse answers from equally intelligent and upright people.

Hume's problem has been to explain, in terms of an account of the nature and origin of human sentiments and passions, both how men come to make moral judgments in general, and how they come to make the particular moral judgments which they do make. As far as the latter point is concerned, he has also to explain the basic similarity or uniformity that he supposes to exist in men's moral judgments and at the same time account for any variations that may occur. His attempt to solve the problem, in the manner which I have outlined, does derive an 'ought' from an 'is', in the sense that it sets out to explain how men are led, through certain permanent features of human nature and the human situation, to make moral judgments which involve attitudes of praise and blame. But it is not, obviously at least, an attempt to *deduce* an 'ought' from an 'is': Hume does not seem to be saying 'The facts about human nature are such-and-such; therefore men ought to behave in certain ways' so much as 'The facts about human nature are such-and-such, and these facts cause men to judge that they ought to behave in certain ways'. Of course he is a human being as well as a philosopher, and as such he makes moral judgments according to what he regards as the normal principles on which such judgments are made; but on the whole he does not consider the philosopher to be qualified by his special occupation to have an insight into moral truth denied to his less fortunate brethren (and why should he, when morality is a matter of sentiment, not of reason?). Hume is trying to explain the phenomena of morality: he is a descriptive moralist, not a normative one. He is a naturalist, not because he does something that hostile critics can condemn as committing the naturalistic fallacy in some form or other, but, quite simply, because he finds the key to the description and explanation of the moral judgments men actually make in the basic facts of human nature, not in the supernatural realms of theology nor in the *a priori* categories of rationally determined fitnesses and unfitnesses of things.

NOTES

1. The point here is presumably that men, like many animals, may have a natural and instinctive desire to promote the well-being of those who are closely connected with them by ties of blood relationship; but there is no such instinctive desire for the welfare of other human beings *qua* human beings.

2. In the earlier *Elements of Law* and *De Cive* Hobbes had attached much greater importance to glory as a motivating force; in the theory of *Leviathan*, although it is still mentioned, it plays a very small part – quite rightly, since the desire for reputation and position varies enormously from man to man and from society to society, and cannot properly be regarded as a fundamental motive of all human conduct.

3. Whether we say 'take the steps necessary' or 'take the steps which he thinks necessary' (Hobbes sometimes says one, and sometimes the other) is not important in this context; for as long as we are considering a man's natural, as opposed to civil or political, rights, the individual himself is the only judge as to the suitability or necessity of any given means to the required end.

4. Cp. especially T. Nagel, 'Hobbes's Conception of Obligation', *Philosophical Review*, 68 (1959) 68–83.

5. The best statement of the theological interpretation of Hobbes's argument is to be found in A. E. Taylor, 'The Ethical Doctrine of Hobbes', *Philosophy* (1938), and the best criticism of the interpretation in Stuart M. Brown Jr, 'The Taylor Thesis: Some Objections', *Philosophical Review* (1959). Both these papers are reprinted in K. C. Brown, ed., *Hobbes Studies* (Oxford, 1965).

6. Hume sometimes speaks of a moral sentiment, sometimes of a moral sense. But the latter is, for him, a misleading way of speaking.

7. The exact interpretation of this passage has given rise to much controversy. See, for example, the essays by A. C. MacIntyre, R. F. Atkinson, Antony Flew, Geoffrey Hunter and W. D. Hudson in the volume on *Hume*, ed. V. C. Chappell, in the Modern Studies in Philosophy series (London, 1968); and also in *The Is–Ought Question*, ed. W. D. Hudson (London, 1969).

BIBLIOGRAPHY

HOBBES

BROWN, K. C. (ed.), *Hobbes Studies* (Oxford, 1965).
LAIRD, J., *Hobbes* (London, 1934).
MCNEILLY, F. S., *The Anatomy of Leviathan* (London, 1968).
PETERS, R., *Hobbes* (Harmondsworth, 1956).
PRIOR, A. N., *Logic and the Basis of Ethics* (Oxford, 1949).
ROBERTSON, G. C., *Hobbes* (Edinburgh, 1886).
WARRENDER, H., *The Political Philosophy of Hobbes* (Oxford, 1957).
WATKINS, J. W. N., *Hobbes's System of Ideas* (London, 1965).

HUME

ÁRDAL, P. S., *Passion and Value in Hume's Treatise* (Edinburgh, 1966).
BROILES, R. D., *The Moral Philosophy of David Hume* (The Hague, 1964).
CHAPPELL, V. C. (ed.), *Hume* (London, 1968).
KEMP SMITH, N., *The Philosophy of David Hume* (London, 1941).
LAIRD, J., *Hume's Philosophy of Human Nature* (London, 1932).
MACNABB, D. G. C., *David Hume: His Theory of Knowledge and Morality*, 2nd ed. (Oxford, 1966).
PEARS, D. F. (ed.), *David Hume: a Symposium* (London, 1963).
STEWART, J. B., *The Moral and Political Philosophy of David Hume* (New York, 1963).